essentials

80/20 Management

Time-saving books that teach specific skills to busy people, focusing on what really matters; the things that make a difference – the *essentials*.

Other books in the series include:

Leading Teams

Boost Your Word Power

Coaching People

Hiring People

Solving Problems

Delegating

Writing Good Reports

Making the Most of Your Time

Business Letters that Work

Writing, Speaking, Listening

80/20 Management

Julie-Ann Amos

ESSENTIALS

Published in 2001 by
How To Books Ltd, 3 Newtec Place,
Magdalen Road, Oxford OX4 1RE, United Kingdom
Tel: (01865) 793806 Fax: (01865) 248780
email: info@howtobooks.co.uk
www.howtobooks.co.uk

First published 2001
This edition specially printed in 2002
for the Institute of Leadership & Management

British Library Cataloguing in Publication Data.
A catalogue record for this book is available from
the British Library.

Edited by Diana Brueton
Cover design by Shireen Nathoo Design, London
Produced for How To Books by Deer Park Productions
Designed and typeset by Shireen Nathoo Design, London
Printed and bound in Great Britain by Bell & Bain Ltd, Glasgow

ESSENTIALS *is an imprint of*
How To Books

Contents

Preface **7**

1 Introduction to 80/20 Management **9**
Pareto's rule 11
The 80% factor 12
The 20% factor 14
Management essentials 15

2 80/20 Time Management and Delegation **17**
Prioritising 19
Managing your time 22
Managing other people's time 26
Delegating 30

3 80/20 Problem-Solving and Decision-Making **35**
Problem-solving 37
Creativity 40
Decision-making 44

4 80/20 Recruitment and Training **47**
Recruitment 49
Selection 53
Induction 56
Training 59

5 80/20 Teamwork and Performance 63
Leadership 65
Teamwork 68
Motivation and performance problems 70
Meetings 77

6 80/20 People Problems and Change Management 81
Grievances 83
Discipline 85
Handling change 89
Helping others through change 93

Preface

In management, what you do and the way you do it are vital to your success. Yet all too often we find ourselves dealing with trivia and time-consuming tasks, or doing tasks in a complex and time-consuming manner. Why?

Pareto's rule states that 80% of results comes from 20% of effort. But identifying that all-important 20% on which we should be focusing is a skill we need to keep in mind constantly if we are to succeed. It's all too easy to slip into spending time on activities that are unproductive.

This book aims to help you get the balance right with your work, so you can see where to apply effort for maximum effect. It is more than just a book on the essentials of management – it is designed to concentrate on the 20% of tasks and activities that will have most effect on your workload and working life. The book also aims to show you a few ways to help you ignore or get rid of the 80% of tasks and activities that are a distraction and drain on your precious time and energy. Good luck!

Julie-Ann Amos

1 Introduction to 80/20 Management

You don't just wade in and start working through your tasks – you have to stop and evaluate. What's important? What's urgent? What's overdue?

In this chapter, four things that really matter:

~ **Pareto's rule**

~ **The 80% factor**

~ **The 20% factor**

~ **Management essentials**

All too often in today's workplace we find ourselves too busy: overloaded with work; stretched at the seams; frustrated with never having the time to do work to the best of our ability. Sounds familiar? Management isn't easy, and it's all too often full of frustration. Identifying the main tasks which drive and facilitate your overall purpose at work is essential if you are to keep on top of things.

80/20 management is based on Pareto's rule – that 20% of effort achieves 80% of results. In 80/20 management we simply try to focus on identifying the 20% of tasks and activities that will produce the most results, and work on those as a priority.

Of course, spending as much time as possible on these tasks shouldn't leave your other work undone – the trick is to keep on top of things by shifting your priorities subtly towards the 20% of tasks and activities that will lever the maximum impact for you. *

Is this you?

If I stopped to think about what to do before I started, I'd have less time to work! • I have a checklist of tasks and priorities; isn't that enough? • I don't really know what things are *most* important in my job, I just get on with it and keep my head down. • Anything that makes me feel less overwhelmed in peak times would be a bonus!

** That way you maximise the impact and results from what you do spend your time on.*

Pareto's rule

Pareto's rule is a principle of time management. It basically tells us you need to spend time on actually *doing* things – i.e. achieving – not just being busy. Anyone can be busy, the trick is to be busy doing the *right* things.

At one time or another we've all got stuck in to a busy workload with little planning and discrimination. But working like this means people often spend as much time doing minor, irrelevant tasks as they do on the really important things. What is worse, some people spend even more time on the unimportant things than on important tasks!

Pareto's rule states that 20% of effort actually achieves 80% of results. Of course, these numbers aren't precise, but typically 80% of time spent actually achieves very little (20% of results).

What does this mean? Put simply, if most of the time we spend is wasted – in that it is producing little result – then focusing on the aspects of our work that *do* yield most results will make us enormously more productive. Applying Pareto's rule to management, this book tries to focus on the important things in management: the things that will constitute a large part of the 20% which will bring most people the most benefit.

This book focuses on what should, for most people, constitute the 20% of really important core activities of management that will achieve the most for you. *

** If 20% of your time produces 80% of your results, 80% of your time is wasted or ill-used. What to focus on at any given time is therefore a crucial decision to make.*

The 80% factor

Taking Pareto's rule, it would be helpful to identify the 80% of your work that produces least reward. But what then? You need to take things a stage further and think about how to reduce that 80% as much as possible.

- **Delegate** where you can. Chapter 2 deals with the essentials of delegation, which doesn't mean simply farming your own work out to others! First, you need to plan the delegation and invest time in making sure the other people can cope, before eventually stepping back and letting them get on with it, releasing your time. You will need to invest time to make time.

- **Negotiate** with other people as to whether tasks are really necessary, especially routine ones such as regular meetings and reports, updates etc. Find out how often these tasks are really needed, if at all, and identify ways of streamlining them so they take less time and effort. Can they be done less often? Can the tasks be delegated? Again, you will need to invest time getting things organised to save time later.
- **Stop** and see what happens! You'd be surprised how much work we do that isn't actually necessary. Be prepared to go into action quickly, however, if stopping a task *does* cause a problem.
- **Postpone** routine tasks or similar tasks so they are all done at the same time to similar deadlines. This technique is called *batching* – doing things in batches. It

means you can get groups of tasks over with at regular intervals and forget about them in the meantime. It makes your workload less scattered and piecemeal, which makes it easier for you to concentrate on more important tasks.

The 20% factor

The 20% factor is what this book focuses on. Nobody is saying that all the areas covered in the book added together make up 20% of your time! But for most managers, the 20% of things that have most impact and generate most result will be what is covered here. These areas are the essentials of management.

By focusing on doing these as well as possible, you will achieve maximum gain in your performance. All these areas are important things for managers to be aware of, but by focusing on improving them, you are highly likely to be focusing on improving your performance. *

** You can't be good at everything. Seeking to improve or concentrate on everything is a hopeless task. Eliminate worrying about everything and focus on the most important things.*

Management essentials

This book contains the management essentials. First it covers individual skills such as time management, planning, decision-making and problem-solving. Then it moves on to look at people skills, from recruitment and selection right through to dealing with people problems. The aim is to give you assistance with core management skills.

Why are these areas in the 20% category? Put simply, they are the areas that usually achieve most impact, and will therefore reap you the most reward if done well.

Efficiency and effectiveness

Efficiency and effectiveness are linked to Pareto's rule. Efficiency is doing things well. Effectiveness is doing the right things – i.e. the 20%. Essential management is being good at both – doing the right things in the best way. This is how you can achieve maximum results from minimum effort. It's called *leveraging* your time and effort. *

*** Good management comes not from one area, but from being competent at a whole range of management essentials.***

Summary points

★ Understand Pareto's rule.

★ Identify tasks and activities in the 80% category, and move towards eliminating or reducing these as much as possible.

★ Identify tasks in the 20% category and work on maximising your time and effort spent on these.

★ No one is saying the 80% /20% split is a fact – it's a concept. By using it you will concentrate more on management essentials, and that in turn will make you better at managing yourself and others.

2 80/20 Time Management and Delegation

Prioritising your own time and leveraging other people's will relieve pressure on you so that you can concentrate on the major issues.

In this chapter, four things that really matter:

~ **Prioritising**

~ **Managing your time**

~ **Managing other people's time**

~ **Delegating**

Managing your time is a skill, but it has limited ability to help you through peak periods and make a real impact on your workloads. The ability to also manage other people's time, and especially to delegate, is a far more efficient and effective proposition.

If you are not careful, however, you can leave people feeling put upon, and manipulated and you will often strain working relationships. When dealing with others, you need to be sensitive and careful.

Delegating is an especially emotive issue. Some people relish being delegated to; others hate it. It is one of the most important factors in freeing up your own time, but it takes time and effort to start the process in the first place. Only then can you reap the very real rewards. Managing your own and other people's time is a skill that will impact not only you but those around you, so everyone benefits. *

Is this you?

Come off it! People spend so much time managing their time that they never get any real work done! • If I delegate my work, what will people think I do all day? • It's wrong to try to manage other people's time – it's thinly disguised manipulation. • I get by pretty well – why do I need to plan and think about managing my time? I get the job done, after all.

*** Then you can decide what priorities to concentrate on during the time you have made available.***

Prioritising

Prioritising is relatively simple – just be aware that important tasks are not necessarily urgent and vice versa. Assess each task separately for its:

~ **Importance** – these are tasks that need to be done right, they are quality-related. They are the tasks in the 20% category.

~ **Urgency** – these are tasks that are time-related, not quality-related.

This is a simple view assuming all tasks can be done in one sitting, but of course tasks are often large and complex, or even whole projects consisting of a whole range of tasks. This is why it is vital that you establish a list of *everything* you have to do, and work from there. That way, sub-tasks or stages of larger or more complex tasks can each be treated as tasks in their own right, and given deadlines to enable you to meet any overall project deadline. This is the basis on which project management works. It will allow the *importance vs urgency* prioritising to work effectively, so everything gets done when it needs to.

This will give you four categories of task:

	Important	**Not important**
Urgent	*First.* Do it *now*!	*Second.* Do it quickly
Not urgent	*Third.* Do it carefully	*Last.* Don't do it!

First – do it now

These are tasks which are both important and urgent. Urgency dictates that they are done immediately, but their importance dictates that you spend sufficient time on them to do a good job. Not only do you need to do it now, you need to get it right. These are the highest priority tasks you have.

Second – do it quickly

These are tasks which are unimportant but need to be done urgently. Only spend as much time on them as is really necessary – you need to get them out of the way so you have the rest of your time for more important tasks. These come after 'do it now' tasks because they are less important, and missing a deadline for one of these is probably going to land you in less hot water. Alternatively, sometimes it can be better to clear these tasks so that you can focus attention on 'do it now' tasks.

Third – do it carefully

These are important tasks. You need to spend sufficient time on them to make sure they are done well, without rushing them.

Last – don't do it

These tasks are to be left until you have done everything else, and you may even not do them at all. In the longer term, negotiate or arrange to stop these.

But it all takes time!

Remember, a great deal of management is investing time now in activities that will reap you benefits later. Listing and making deadlines for all tasks and planning your priorities takes time, but it is the only way to ensure you don't miss deadlines, or rush important work. *

Managing your time

Why manage your time? Good time management can improve your:

- ~ time available to do what you want
- ~ decision-making
- ~ health / stress levels
- ~ productivity / efficiency
- ~ effectiveness
- ~ quality of life
- ~ working relationships.

Sounds impressive, doesn't it? Managing your time involves more than just prioritising, however. It also involves setting limits, making decisions about how you spend your time, and scheduling (*when* to do things).

**** Doing the right things in the right order can save you a lot of time and effort.***

Setting limits

- **Limit availability** – by responding, not reacting to requests. How urgent is it, really? Do you need to be accessible at all times? Can you have 'closed door' or 'do not disturb' times? Do you really need to deal with interruptions then and there? Not limiting availability places you at the beck and call of everyone willing to interrupt you.
- **Limit durations** – by refusing to spend large amounts of time on unimportant work. The reason why Pareto's rule works is because people don't limit the amount of time they spend on unimportant tasks. Set limits for how long to spend doing something, and if it isn't finished within that time, ask whether you should really continue with it.
- **Limit importance** – not all our work is important. Believing so is simply a tactic to make *ourselves* feel important, but even if it were true, there are degrees of importance. Check your assumptions – is

all work from a particular person really important? Does a deadline mean it's important, or is it just urgent?

- **Limit involvement** – in things that don't produce many benefits. Being involved in too many matters drains our time and energy. Limit your involvement to activities you *need* to be involved in. Delegation reduces your own involvement over time.
- **Limit standards** – check the standard required for a task, and make sure you aren't being a perfectionist. Doing good work is all very well, but if it is at the expense of something else, you will suffer for it eventually. Do things *well enough*, and save your high standards for really important work.
- **Limit urgency** – It's easy to overemphasise work's urgency – it makes us feel important to be rushing around in demand. But giving priority to non-urgent work means less time available, and

possibly rushing work that should be done more carefully.

Spending time

~ Spend time on the right things – by prioritising.

~ Spend time doing what you like doing where possible, – you will feel happier and get more done.

~ Spend time doing what you're good at – this is efficient, and will also make you feel good, as it will fuel your sense of achievement.

~ Spend time achieving results – not putting in effort. This is the essence of Pareto's rule.

~ Spend time at the right time – some people work best at certain times, and some tasks are best done at certain times. Try to do work at the best time – for it and you! eg plan work which requires alertness for early in the day, and work that needs peace and quiet late in the day when there are fewer interruptions. *

*** Managing your time is essential to get everything done efficiently and effectively.***

Managing other people's time

Managing other people is not the easiest task in the world, and managing how they spend their time can be very difficult without offending them. How we choose to spend our time is very personal, and people may resent being organised.

In spite of this, it is essential that you exert at least some control over the time of others, in that it impacts on you and your own time usage. Let's look at the main problems with managing other people's time.

Perfectionism

Some people are perfectionists. They like to give attention to detail and to produce quality work. Most workplaces value accuracy, it's true, but perfectionism can interfere with progress if it gets out of hand. Perfectionists regard everything as important, so it's hard to get them to work quickly. Sometimes they may let you down and not produce work at all if they can't get it right – doing nothing may seem better to them than doing poor quality work!

~ Reassure that mistakes are acceptable.

~ Keep reminding people about deadlines.

~ Set detailed standards for work, to avoid ridiculously high standards.

~ Focus on achieving the task, not the quality.

~ Do not reward over-achievement, as this can encourage perfectionism to become worse.

~ Check progress regularly.

~ Be open about your own mistakes so failure is less feared.

~ Openly discuss priorities, and make sure people work to the right ones.

Procrastination

Procrastination means putting things off. Procrastinators are easily distracted and can ignore things until the last minute. Low priority tasks can get in the way of high priority ones.

~ Break tasks down into steps with people so they don't feel intimidated by large or complex tasks. Sub-tasks with deadlines are especially good.

~ Monitor progress, enabling achievement to be watched along the way. Tick lists add to a sense of achievement and make the overall task less intimidating.

~ Confront it – ask why they are delaying getting started. If you can get to the bottom of their thinking, you can deal with it.

~ Reward progress.

~ Remove all possible distractions.

Interruptions

Interruptions are part of life, but managing them effectively can save you a great deal of time and disruption.

~ Allow a certain amount of time for interruptions, as you know they'll happen anyway.

~ Don't be too welcoming – people need to know you're busy.

~ Look briefly at a watch or clock when they interrupt. It implies quite politely that you are working to a deadline, and they are more likely to keep things brief.

~ Set and publicise an 'open door' time, when you are happy to receive callers. It discourages people from interrupting you at other times, and if they do you can ask them to return during the 'open door'.

~ Stand up when people interrupt you. It gives a very clear indication that they are taking you away from your work, and also discourages them from sitting down, which means they tend to stay longer.

~ When you're interrupted, don't stop what you are doing immediately – make them wait a few moments. This reinforces the message that they are stopping you working on something important. *

** There's a lot you can do to manage other people and the way they impinge on your own time.*

Delegating

Advantages for you

~ More time.

~ Freedom to concentrate on other things.

~ Protection if you are away – people being able to carry on with parts of your work.

Advantages for others

~ Skills development.

~ Ability to use existing skills more fully.

~ Involvement, which increases morale and motivation.

~ Less delays as they have freedom to make decisions themselves.

Identifying delegation tasks

It's actually easiest to identify tasks for delegation by identifying and excluding all the tasks that you *can't* delegate! These are:

~ Tough tasks – beyond the skills and/or capabilities of the people concerned.

~ Never ever take a task away and give it to someone else – it's humiliating.

Review

After the task is over, review and give them feedback. This is rewarding and they will feel more motivated. Even if things went badly, people will feel better if you reassure them. *

ion is not ken It is a fine between g control sponsibility, ving away m and ntability.

Summary points

★ Make time to establish your priorities before starting a task. They will also need revising after each task.

★ Manage your own time so you can work without rushing.

★ Manage other people, or they will impinge on your own time.

★ Invest time in delegating properly, to avoid wasting time solving problems later.

~ Critical tasks – tasks so crucial that failure would cause big problems. It's only acceptable to delegate these if you are absolutely sure they won't fail!

~ Delegated tasks – assume that someone has a reason for delegating to you, so don't pass these on without permission.

You will typically be left with things which are fine to delegate, such as :

~ Routine tasks

~ Easy tasks

~ Time-consuming tasks

~ Non-urgent tasks

~ Parts of more complex tasks

Who to delegate to

~ People with spare time

~ Juniors, so they feel they are progressing

~ Senior staff, so they gain status

- People with the necessary skills
- People who want to learn new skills

Just ask yourself the following questions, and never underestimate the last one – giving people work they hate won't gain you any friends and will make people reluctant to take on tasks from you in future.

- Do they have the time for the task?
- Do they have the ability?
- If not, can you train or coach them?
- Would they enjoy it?

Communicate

- **Communicate the task** – precisely. Explain why you are delegating it.
- **Communicate the limits** – explain how much accountability you are giving them. What support, help, advice, resources and training are you making available?
- **Communicate to others** – so everyone

knows you a
that they sh
backing.

- **Communicat deadlines** – s about the task them. A good setting objecti

Let them get on

- Give support wi freedom to do th
- Monitor progress without constant
- Intervene only wh preferably not at a obviously wrong, l problems – not the
- Never take back a ta better to work with necessary.

Delega to be t lightly. balanc keepin and re and g freedo accou

3 80/20 Problem-Solving and Decision-Making

People don't always come up with the right answer first time. Good decisions and solutions to problems take time and effort.

In this chapter, three things that really matter:

~ **Problem-solving**

~ **Creativity**

~ **Decision-making**

Problem-solving, creativity and decision-making are inextricably linked. To solve any problem you will usually have to think it through and generate a number of potential ideas or solutions. This involves creativity in some shape or form. Eventually you will pick your solution by making a decision.

The main skills involved in problem-solving, therefore, are actually creativity and decision-making! There are tried and tested ways to help you generate ideas and options, so you have sufficient courses of action from which to choose.

All too often people see a problem and make a decision about how to resolve it. They don't actually look at solving the problem in any depth. They don't spend time exploring possibilities. They just decide what to do. The decision may work, it may even work well, but by being hasty and thinking short-term it will rarely be the best decision that could have been made. *

Is this you?

Most of my problems are things I can solve straight away. • I don't need the best solution; I can resolve things again later if it doesn't work out. • I often take more time solving the problem than it took up in the first place! • Sometimes I just can't think of new ideas. • How can you solve age-old, recurring problems? Everything has been tried before.

** Making decisions is something anyone can do – but the trick is making the right decisions.*

Problem-solving

Whether to look at problems alone or use other people can be a difficult choice. Both have advantages and disadvantages.

Individual problem-solving

~ An expert usually knows best.

~ It's quicker.

~ Ideas tend to 'dry up' more quickly, limiting options.

~ Narrow thinking can limit ideas.

~ Stress – it can be lonely carrying the responsibility for a decision alone.

Group problem-solving

~ Usually achieves better than average decisions.

~ Discussions can get out of hand.

~ More ideas generated.

~ People can get upset if their idea is rejected.

- Things take longer.
- Solutions tend to be more accurate, and overlook less.

Define the problem or issue

Take time out to think things through, but don't leave it and hope it will go away! Writing out the problem may clarify things.

Problems v solutions

Problems are often actually unwanted solutions, not the problem. The real problem is undefined and underlying. For example, you are asked to reduce customer complaints. So the problem is not reducing complaints – that is the desired solution! The problem is what is causing the complaints? Listing the various potential causes and finding which ones are causing the complaints gives you the real problem, for example poor accuracy of order taking, or an insufficient dispatch check system. *

Keep trying to dig down to find the root of something, which will give you the core problem.

Social *vs* technical

Most problems have two aspects.

- ~ Social aspects are caused by the human factor and people's interactions.
- ~ Technical aspects are caused by technical issues.

In the above example, poor accuracy of order-taking is a social issue, and insufficient dispatch check system is a technical issue.

If the dispatch check system was okay, but people weren't using it properly, that would be social not technical. Similarly, if the order taking was done on a form that wasn't capturing all the necessary information, that would be technical. Not all problems have both aspects, but often they do.

Gathering information

You have to investigate in order to get at the real, underlying cause of any problem. The more information you can gather, the better quality decision you can make. Remember that *facts* are more important pieces of information than *deductions*, or *opinions*.

Beware of procrastination

Some people spend so much time looking for information, checking facts and defining the problem that they never actually get round to doing anything about it. Beware that you don't start to procrastinate.

Logical thinking

Some problems can be solved by analysis and logical thinking alone – they don't need creativity to come up with options. *

Creativity

The purpose of creativity in problem-solving is to increase the number of options and possibilities from which you can eventually make your decision. It has advantages and disadvantages:

Advantages:

~ Options can be generated with little or no facts.

* *The first problem you see is rarely the actual problem – it's an unwanted solution to the real problem, a symptom of the underlying cause.*

- More options can be generated than by using logical deduction alone.
- More factors can be taken into account.

Disadvantages:

- Some people find creative thinking very difficult.
- Options generated may turn out to be wrong if not based on facts.
- People may not take options seriously unless backed by facts and/or data.

Brainstorming

Brainstorming is a creative technique where a number of people (it can be just two) are encouraged to come up with ideas and suggestions, no matter how silly or impractical. Ideas are not judged, criticised or evaluated. People are free to use their imaginations, bouncing ideas around.

All options are recorded, even the impossibly impractical ones, as unworkable ideas can stimulate other ideas, and so on.

Once a large number of ideas has been generated, they can be evaluated and narrowed down to the best suggestions.

Advantages:

~ Produces a large number of options.

~ Motivates people.

~ Fun to do.

Disadvantages:

~ Some people find it difficult.

~ Critical people may upset others.

~ Session leader needs to keep things on track.

~ Can get over-frivolous and high-spirited.

Barriers to creative thinking

~ People have mental blocks – they don't think they are or can be creative.

~ Belief there is only one right answer.

~ People want to conform, so they only produce ideas they think will be acceptable.

- Laziness – accepting the obvious solution, not working to find the best one.
- Hasty evaluation, which doesn't give undeveloped ideas time to come to conclusion.
- People are scared of looking silly or being wrong.

Encouraging creative thinking

There are four main ways:

- **Suspend judgement** – give and allow no criticism.
- **Freewheel** – the wilder the ideas the better.
- **Quality not quantity** – the more ideas the better.
- **Combining** – don't leave ideas as they stand, combine and build on them to make others. *

*** Being creative isn't necessarily something you are, it can be something you do. With practice, it gets easier.***

Decision-making

Evaluating options

When you have options and ideas, you now have to evaluate them, by looking at the advantages and disadvantages, or pros and cons of each. A table of advantages and disadvantages will often make things clearer, especially if there are quite a few options or ideas.

Consider constraints

Always remember to check any constraints on your decision. Constraints such as a maximum budget, or the need to resolve the problem without any increase in staff, will affect which potential solutions are feasible and which are not. There may not be one *right* answer – remember you are looking for the *best* answer, but within limits. Constraints will weed out any *bad* answers!

Priorities

Where you still have several potential solutions and are trying to decide on the best one, try using priorities. Look at your priorities, and rank them in order. Decide which is the most important priority, eg increasing cost, or reducing time. By applying both constraints and priorities, you are likely to find one or two solutions that emerge as definitely better. This gives you the best answer, or at least the ability to choose it from few alternatives. *

Tie up loose ends

Once you have made your decision, remember to tie up all the loose ends:

- Record information and options, to avoid reinventing the wheel in future.
- Communicate the decision and explain the reasons.
- Monitor progress. Check the solution still works after a period of time.
- Thank people who helped.
- Don't be afraid to adjust your decision if necessary.

** If you have nothing to choose between options, use your own criteria or intuition. If all are equally good you can't get it wrong!*

~ Check for other problems that may be caused by your solution – the knock-on effect.

Summary points

★ A structured approach to problem solving will give you the best framework for getting to the real root of an issue.

★ Creativity can be learned and practised. It is not necessarily something you have or you don't have.

★ Make decisions logically once you have the options. Use constraints and priorities to decide, and follow up afterwards.

4 80/20 Recruitment and Training

Recruitment and training are essential, to get people to work for you and to keep them from leaving. Doing it well can make a huge difference to your team when new people join.

In this chapter, four things that really matter:

~ **Recruitment**

~ **Selection**

~ **Induction**

~ **Training**

Recruitment and training are a drain on your time and energy.

Recruitment is not only expensive, it also means that you are missing someone until you get the job filled with a new person, and you have to cover that work until you recruit someone.

Choosing someone isn't easy – the consequences of getting it wrong can cause disaster, so success is crucial.

Once you have found the right person, you are then faced with someone who will be unproductive for a while. No matter how experienced the new person is, everyone takes some time to get to know the ropes. A good induction can help them settle in and be productive quicker. Induction is training to start them off in the new job. Other training will help people improve their performance. *

Is this you?

I hate recruitment – I never know what I'm doing and the risk of choosing the wrong person is so high. • I'm not sure the right person exists – surely you just choose someone competent and then train them about company nuances? • I leave induction to the others. Helping someone new settle in is good for them as a team. • Training is expensive – and I never really see any results.

** The time spent training must be recouped, or it is a pointless exercise.*

Recruitment

Define who and what you want

Consider options such as:

~ Several part-time people instead of one full-time – giving you flexibility.

~ Temporary/fixed term contract people – meaning you don't have to make a firm decision now.

~ Secondment – can someone from another part of the business gain experience from doing the job for a while?

~ Promotion – can you train and promote someone, improving motivation?

~ Redistribution of work – can you redistribute the work and recruit someone with different skills? This can save money.

Job descriptions

Once you have a clear idea in your own mind of what you want, you have your blueprint from which to recruit. Job descriptions are a written outline of the job you want the person to do. You may already have one for the person who has left, but if the job is a new one, you need to write a job description.

Job descriptions should include:

- job title
- department and/or section
- who the jobholder reports to
- purpose of the job/objectives
- duties involved, and methods and standards for carrying these out
- responsibilities for decisions etc
- responsibilities for people, money, equipment etc
- who the job liases with
- where the job is located
- hours of work
- accident or health and safety risks
- salary range
- bonus or incentive schemes if any

- pensions and other benefits
- any other duties clause – a clause requiring the jobholder to carry out any other duties within reason on request – this gives you flexibility to vary duties as necessary.

Person specifications

A person specification is a job description translated into human terms – a blueprint for the sort of person you are looking for. It is very useful in preventing discrimination. You list your requirements or criteria, and ask yourself whether they are **essential** or **desirable**:

Physical factors:

- Physical ability and health.
- Required appearance eg grooming, dress, voice – beware of prejudice.

Skills and knowledge:

- What knowledge and/or skills do they need?

- Any qualifications needed?
- Experience or past training required.
- Length of general work experience required – do they need to be experienced at working life or could they be a school-leaver, for example?

Emotional factors:

- How important is it to get on with others?
- Is any leadership or management required?
- Is stability important?
- Is self-reliance (independent thought and working) required?

Advertising

However you choose to advertise, you will waste time attracting unsuitable applicants if you do not include the essentials: *

- where the job is
- salary or pay

* ***If you don't specify exactly what you want, how will you know when you find it?***

- hours
- essential criteria required
- a date by which to apply
- how they should apply.

Selection

Recruitment is about attracting applicants, whereas selection is choosing the right person from the pool of candidates available.

Selecting a shortlist

Initial selection is relatively easy, because you simply have to compare applicants with the person specification and eliminate all people who do not have all the essential requirements. If this leaves you with a suitable shortlist, fine. If not, eliminate any that have only a small number of your desirable criteria. Keep a note of your deliberations and process in writing for at least six months, to substantiate your decision if anyone complains of unfair treatment such as discrimination. You should also send a polite letter to those you have rejected.

Arranging interviews

Make sure you invite sufficient candidates – they may not all turn up! Give sufficient notice. Make sure interviews will not be disturbed and are in an appropriate room. You also need to arrange somewhere for people to wait before their interview.

Avoiding discrimination

You must not discriminate against particular groups unless the law specifically allows it. Discrimination can be direct or indirect and includes:

- Deliberately excluding people from a particular group.
- Not specifying the same criteria for everyone.
- Setting criteria that people from a particular group are less likely to have.

~ Using criteria or tests that are not necessary for success at the job.

~ Setting tasks for some people but not others.

~ Asking questions of some people but not others.

Purpose of interviewing

~ Interviews should confirm and expand on information you already have.

~ They should give the candidate more information about the job.

Problems with interviews

~ Time – you only have a limited period of time to find out all you need.

~ Stress – the interviewer or the interviewee (or even both) may be under stress or nervous, which can cause one or both of you to behave abnormally.

Key points for interviews

~ Control the interview by questioning.

- Establish rapport to reduce stress.
- Listen and observe.
- Be sensitive.
- Prepare thoroughly.
- Structure the content so you get to ask all you want within the time. *

Induction

When new staff start they need to know many things before they can begin being productive. The longer they take to learn those things, the more distracting or disruptive they are to others, through no fault of their own. To help them contribute as quickly as possible, set time aside for induction.

Most new people leave within the first few weeks if they are going to, so people need to feel part of the team and happy fairly quickly. You may have a company induction course for people, but the most important thing is to make time for the new person. Try to set

*** Choosing the right person isn't actually that difficult – if you are methodical and organised about it.***

aside some time for them every day for a while. Covering all the following areas will ensure anyone gets off to a good start.

Documentation and procedures

~ any timesheets, or signing in and out procedures

~ payday and method of payment

~ any bonus, productivity or incentive schemes

~ what to do in the event of sickness or absence

~ how to book holidays and/or time off

~ any forms they need to sign.

Introductions

~ to colleagues, supervisor/manager

~ to their job and the main duties

~ to contacts outside the immediate workplace

Working arrangements

- ~ the workplace
- ~ hours of work
- ~ tea and coffee breaks and facilities
- ~ canteen/cloakroom/staff room and toilet facilities
- ~ issue of any equipment, tools, uniform etc
- ~ relationships between their own work and that of others.

Emergency and safety

- ~ emergency procedures
- ~ fire precautions and drills
- ~ first aid location
- ~ safety policy, procedures and practices.

General information

- ~ description and structure of section/team, department, organisation
- ~ names of key people

- union or social club membership if applicable
- holidays – entitlements, timings etc
- pension and other pay deductions
- grievances – how to raise them
- disciplinary procedures
- workplace rules and customs
- available training schemes or programmes
- personnel policies.

Training

Why train people?

- To enable them to do the job properly.
- To maintain quality and quantity of work.
- To meet legal requirements (eg health and safety training).
- To give you flexibility.
- To develop them.

- To give someone a boost.
- To prepare for forthcoming changes.

Training needs and objectives

A *training need* is a shortfall in performance that training could correct. Many organisations use appraisals as an opportunity to discuss training needs, but this can mean you only consider training once a year!

Set objectives to fill the needs, which will help you match up your objectives in training the person with the training objectives of the course or training suggested. For example:

Training need – to be able to use a new computer package.

Objective – to be able to use new computer package unsupervised, but with occasional reference to the manual, after training course – *or* to be able to use new computer package with reference to manual after training course, increasing to full competency unaided after six months.

Identifying suitable training

- ~ Can you train them yourself?
- ~ Can someone else in the workplace train them?
- ~ Can they get the information they need from books or manuals?
- ~ Is there a training course?
- ~ Can they learn from working with others who are more experienced?

Commitment

Once training has been arranged, stick to it. * Not only is it expensive to cancel courses at the last minute, but people become disappointed. Plan for training properly so that it takes place when scheduled.

Evaluation

Evaluate after training – don't assume that because they have attended all is well. Check whether or not the objective has been fulfilled. If not, you may have to look at additional training and/or support.

** Training is not a necessary evil; it is something that can greatly improve productivity and quality of work.*

Summary points

★ Define exactly who and what you want before starting to recruit. Don't assume you need to replace like with like.

★ Use criteria to shortlist and make your selection. Process objective.

★ Induct new employees properly – they are at their most vulnerable in the first few weeks.

★ When training needs are identified, commit to appropriate training and stick to it.

5 80/20 Teamwork and Performance

You have a massive influence on people just by being "the boss". Teamwork and leadership skills don't always come naturally though, and sometimes need work.

In this chapter, four things that really matter:

~ **Leadership**

~ **Teamwork**

~ **Motivation and performance problems**

~ **Meetings**

Teamwork and leadership go hand in hand. You can't be a leader without a team, and most teams will need a leader at some stage. Understanding effective leadership and good teamwork is essential if you want to lead your own team well. People will look to you as a leader whether or not you try to be a good one, so avoiding your responsibility here won't help.

When things go wrong in a team, and

motivation suffers or performance declines for some reason, this is when a leader needs to make some tough decisions. It is usually necessary to step in and handle the situation in some way – otherwise it can spread to other team members and maybe even the whole team.

Meetings are a particular situation where a team of people get together, with a leader running the meeting. They are something which many people find wastes time and is unproductive, but handled well, they can be both enjoyable and a huge boost to efficiency.

Is this you?

I'm the boss. Good or bad, my team has to toe the line anyway. • I'm simply not a born leader. • Teamwork is all very well but most of my people prefer to work on their own and just get on with it. • Motivation comes from within. I can't do anything to make someone motivated! • I hate meetings. They're such a waste, and nothing ever comes of them.

Leadership

Management is about being in charge, controlling, administering, handling (according to the dictionary!). Leadership is being the principal, or front-runner, holding the chief role. Leadership is a visible role, and leaders tend to be elected or chosen, whereas managers tend to be appointed. *

** For example, if a manager doesn't lead their team well, it will often find its own leader from within.*

Leadership expectations

In a crisis people usually look to someone to take control. They generally seek someone with:

~ position (status)

~ personality (charisma)

~ expertise or experience.

Leadership traits

In addition to having one or more of the above, there are definitely ways in which you can become a better leader. One way of improving your leadership skills is to identify the traits of successful leaders and try to improve these in yourself. This is called modelling – identify a leader you would like to resemble, and ask what traits they have and use. Trying to improve these in yourself should make you a better leader. Of course, some traits you are born with, and you can't do much if you don't have them! Others you can work to develop. Here is a list which is not exhaustive:

~ ability to see opportunities
~ adaptability
~ analysis
~ communication
~ decision-making
~ dependability
~ enthusiasm
~ imagination
~ integrity
~ open-mindedness
~ positive thinking
~ reliability
~ sincerity
~ single-mindedness
~ understanding
~ willingness.

Improving your leadership in other ways

~ take advantage of available training

~ keep updated about things going on around you

~ check out areas you are weak in

~ keep in close contact with your own boss

~ learn to work with staff representatives and people with influence

~ get to know other managers and build relationships

~ think ahead and be adaptable – anticipate likely events and plan for them

~ set standards and maintain them

~ monitor and evaluate performance

~ set realistic and achievable objectives for yourself and others

~ encourage involvement, cooperation and compromise in the team

~ keep people informed of progress

- delegate wherever possible
- recognise people's achievements and contributions. *

Teamwork

What makes teams good

- Creativity – usually better than individuals.
- Produce more ideas.
- Can give more opportunities for learning and development.
- Motivates people.
- Shared responsibility, so individuals feel more committed.
- Energy and excitement tends to be greater than working alone.
- Team spirit – a sense of belonging and pride.
- Teams contain a greater range of experience and abilities than any one individual.

** You don't have to be a born leader – there is a lot you can do to improve your chances.*

- Experience and abilities can be used fully.
- Things are quicker: "many hands make light work".
- Productivity is higher.
- A wider range of work can be done.
- They evaluate ideas from many viewpoints, so ideas are better scrutinised.
- Analysis and judgement are usually more objective as all points of view are taken into account.

Team size

The size of a team will affect its performance.

- **Vulnerability** – the smaller the team, the more vulnerable it is. Replacing just one team member can upset an entire small team, and one absence can be critical. In larger teams substitutions and absences can be more easily handled.
- **Relationships** – the smaller the team, the closer the relationships between members. The larger the team, the less

close, and the more danger of small sub-teams developing, which can form a clique, which is exclusive and divides team loyalty.

- **Individuality** – the larger the team, the greater the pressure for conformity and so people have less individuality. Large teams can take on mob mentality. This can mean people stop thinking for themselves and just go along with the team regardless.
- **Control** – the larger the team, the harder it is to control. With large teams, you may need to consider creating sub-groups and a structure, to avoid losing control of parts of the team anyway. *

** Teamwork needs work to make it effective. You can't just expect a group of people to work together effectively.*

Motivation and performance problems

Motivation

Motivation is what makes people act in a particular way. This is important to understand, because if you can identify *why* people do things, it is easier to persuade them to do the things *you* want them to do, or things they wouldn't normally want to do! Motivation makes it far easier to get things done.

Needs

Everyone has needs. A need is a lack of something we want – this produces a drive or motive to satisfy that need. Needs are the key to understanding motivation. Obviously any theory is a simplification, because people often work or are motivated by a combination of needs, but Alderfer categorised needs into three groups:

- existence needs – to maintain us physically
- relatedness needs – to relate to others
- growth needs – to develop and grow as individuals.

Here are some tips on how to motivate people. Which will apply best depends on what needs people have.

Motivating people by filling existence needs

~ Pay people appropriately.

~ Make sure work is safe and pleasant.

~ Give people enough to do.

~ Give incentives, or at the very least recognition for good work.

~ Recognise privacy needs – give people their own space.

~ Try to arrange for people to see the end result of their effort.

~ Set goals so people know what they're doing.

~ Treat people as individuals.

Motivating people by filling relatedness needs

~ Show respect – listen to people and express an interest in them.

~ Give responsibility – delegate.

- Communicate and exchange information openly.
- Encourage ideas and suggestions and involve them in decision making.
- Praise people for effort as well as achievement – something does not have to be perfect to be praised and sometimes failure takes far more effort than success!
- Get to know people and help them get to know others.

Motivating people by filling growth needs

- Offer help and support with new tasks.
- Make work interesting.
- Encourage people to think for themselves.
- Keep people informed about new information and developments.
- Ask people what motivates them and try to give them the chance to do it.
- Give people a change of work or challenge

to stretch them occasionally.

- Offer training where possible.

Signs of demotivation

- increased sickness and/or absence
- lateness
- poor quality work
- lack of communication
- attitude
- emotional levels rise

Reasons for demotivation

- needs not being filled
- boredom/lack of interest or stimulation
- lack of involvement
- not being listened to
- lack of encouragement or recognition
- lack of training
- poor or no delegation

~ criticism

~ too much or too little work.

Dealing with poor performance

Identify the gap

Specify the gap between expected and actual performance. Get them to agree the gap exists if possible. Prove the existence of the gap by:

~ complaints or testimony of others

~ comparisons with others

~ record cards or time sheets

~ errors or rejected work

~ sickness/absence records

~ training needs analysis

~ unfinished work.

Establish reasons for the gap

Establish reasons for the gap, and whether or not they lie within their control, your control, both or neither. Possible reasons include:

- domestic circumstances
- emotional problems
- job changes
- lack of ability
- lack of motivation
- lack of training
- lack of understanding
- personality clashes
- poor discipline
- poor health
- poor management
- poor pay
- under or over confidence
- unreliable equipment.

Close the gap

Set objectives to close the gap. This will bring them up to the required level of performance. You may need to set stages of improvement, each with objectives. If the gap is not closed by the agreed time, you may need to consider disciplinary action. *

Meetings

The formula for a successful meeting is:

Agenda + participation = results

Preparation

- ~ Produce an agenda.
- ~ Do your homework – have items arisen before?

Setting agendas

- ~ Agendas do not need to be formal, they just need to show where the meeting will be, who is required to attend and a list of items to be dealt with.
- ~ First item is usually discussion of the last meeting and any notes or minutes produced.
- ~ Last item is usually any other business.

** Performance issues are solved by simply proving a gap exists, and arranging for it to be filled or closed.*

~ Agendas must be sent out early enough so people can prepare if necessary.

~ Be realistic – not too many items.

~ Give purpose – to the meeting and each item. Any item can be to inform, to consult or to make a decision.

~ Consider a time limit for items, to make sure you tackle all the items and the meeting doesn't overrun.

~ Allow more time for important subjects, or contentious issues.

~ Issue papers in advance where necessary.

Participation

~ **Introductions** – introduce people, including yourself if necessary. Introduce each item briefly.

~ **Motivate** – make sure quiet people are involved and encourage contributions from all. Remain balanced and fair to all.

~ **Listen** – nod, look at people, ask questions. Always try to see others' points of view.

Listen to the minority.

Control

~ Above all else, people expect the chairperson to control a meeting.

~ Control timings.

~ Control contributions, especially proposals, and keep track of discussion.

~ Steer discussions where necessary.

~ Control through courtesy.

~ Do not allow multiple meetings to start, as these are very distracting.

~ Know when to give in, to maintain your integrity as chairperson.

Summarise

~ Sum up periodically.

~ Summarise at the end of a meeting. This is a chance to smooth any ruffled feathers, thank people, and remind people of agreed actions, tasks and responsibilities.

Taking minutes

~ Avoid taking your own minutes, so you can control what goes on and what is written down.

~ Minutes do not have to be formal. *

Summary points

★ Leadership isn't something you are born with – there is a lot you can do to improve skills and abilities.

★ Teamwork is a powerful tool for getting work done, but be alert to potential problems.

★ Understanding motivation means you can keep people motivated and avoid problems. Where problems occur, act to close the gap quickly.

★ Managing meetings is a skill that can be learned. It is not as complex as it seems, either.

** Meetings can be hell, but with good leadership/ chairing skills they can be enjoyable, effective and efficient.*

6 80/20 People Problems and Change Management

You don't always have plain sailing. Situations change, people will have complaints and problems and you may have to take disciplinary action. Good management skills make life a lot easier during the difficult times.

In this chapter, four things that really matter:

~ **Grievances**

~ **Discipline**

~ **Handling change**

~ **Helping others through change**

Managing when things are going well isn't too difficult. But when things get hard, and problems and difficulties arise, this is often the real test of a manager's skills.

Disciplinary and grievance procedures are never easy and, when you are in charge, it's a big responsibility to make sure that everything runs smoothly. More often than not someone will end up feeling they have lost out or been sided against. Handling this can be hard for even the best managers.*

Managing change is a similar area – change can often bring out the worst in people, which causes its own problems. Managing change for yourself and others can help things run more smoothly. If nothing else, it can make people feel better, and that's never a bad thing to achieve.

Is this you?

Why can't people keep their gripes to themselves? I don't want to get involved. • Disciplinary procedures are a last resort – like when you need to fire someone. • Personnel should take charge of disciplinary matters, in my opinion. • Change is inevitable. Why can't people just accept it? • Why should I nursemaid people? I've got my own problems to worry about.

** You can't always be perceived as fair and reasonable, and this can be wearing to cope with.*

Grievances

A *grievance* is a formal or official complaint. Whether made verbally or in writing, these should be taken seriously. Of course we all face grumbles from people, but a formal grumble must be acted upon. Most organisations have a grievance procedure to be followed. In any event there are certain steps that will help.

Listen

Listen carefully and seriously. Grievances are always a situation where feelings are running high, so even if the matter seems silly to you, treat it seriously and you may just enable the person to feel better so they withdraw the matter. Acknowledge the situation – this doesn't mean you agree, just acknowledge what they have said.

Check seriousness

Check whether the person intends to make a formal grievance. Never down-play a complaint in the hope that they will go away

– this is not dealing with things and you may inadvertently end up being part of the problem. Never try to persuade them or dissuade them – just ask whether they want the complaint to be official. Sometimes people just want to sound off to someone, and in the heat of the moment they can dissipate enough of their feelings to feel happier without the need to take things further. If they wish to proceed with a formal grievance, however, this is their right.

Investigate

You need to be completely objective and investigate whether or not the complaint is well founded. You needn't tell the person there is a grievance against them, just try to establish the facts first, because if people feel under threat or suspicion they often get defensive, and you might hear a slightly different version of events. Investigation should be completely objective and neutral.

Take action

Once you have investigated, decide whether

or not the complaint is well founded. If it is, take action, and do this directly with the source of the complaint if possible. If the complaint is unfounded, take action to prove this to the employee making the grievance, or they will feel they have been unfairly treated.

Feedback

Always tell the person making the grievance what you have or are going to do, and why. * You do not need to give details, you can just say that you are dealing officially with the employee concerned and leave it at that. You must do this even if you are taking no action. Preferably, give them feedback in writing.

** Grievances are about feeling unfairly treated. They are about feelings. Always remember to be sympathetic to this and they will be easier to handle.*

Discipline

Disciplinary procedures

Most organisations have a procedure within which you will need to operate. These procedures usually follow a series of stages, such as, typically:

- **Informal warning** – a verbal talk about the situation.
- **Verbal warning** – usually the first stage of formal procedures. A note saying that a verbal warning has been issued should be placed on the employee's file or record.
- **Written warning** – a written warning is given to the employee and a copy placed on their file or record.
- **Final warning** – this is a written warning stating that any further occurrence of the problem will lead to dismissal.
- **Dismissal** – this is a last resort – the employee is dismissed. It usually follows a written warning, but most disciplinary procedures allow for instant or summary dismissal for a very serious breach of discipline regardless of whether or not other stages have been gone through.

Preventing disciplinary problems

- Be approachable – to find out about problems before they get too serious.

- Be consistent and fair.
- Ensure people know all the rules and standards.
- Establish good relationships with people.
- Feed back regularly, and let people know how they are doing **before** a problem becomes serious.
- Foster teamwork.
- Give recognition where it is due.
- Set a good example.
- Set targets and make people aware of them.
- Train people adequately for what is required of them.

Dealing with disciplinary problems

- Know the procedures and your part in them.
- Know the limits of your authority.
- If in doubt at any time, adjourn and take

advice or discuss things with someone else.

- Nip things in the bud wherever possible.
- Deal with things in private – never discipline or tell someone off in front of others.
- Don't put things off because they may get unpleasant.
- Never rush things – give people a chance to speak up for themselves.
- Put a time limit on improvement – set a date.
- Stay calm and objective.
- If you get frustrated or angry, adjourn until you are calm again.
- Be prepared – have information and facts.
- Be prepared to prove there is a problem, if they deny it.
- Focus on the problem, not personalities.
- Get them to talk to you.

~ Keep written records of everything. *

After disciplinary action

~ People will feel under scrutiny – be sensitive.

~ Monitor things without breathing down people's necks.

~ Praise improvement.

~ If there is insufficient improvement by the given deadline, be prepared to escalate the disciplinary process.

Handling change

Changes in employment, technology, finance, legislation and many other areas of our lives are constantly challenging us. Changes occur on many different levels.

Routine change (everyday changes)

These are the sorts of changes managers face every day. Routine changes cause routine problem-solving exercises. They may

** Disciplinary matters are very serious indeed – they can affect someone's career. Treat them seriously, and be fair and objective at all times.*

require big decisions, or cost a great deal of money, but they are the sort of things that crop up from time to time or regularly at work. Examples might be a resignation, equipment failure, or a complaint.

Emergency change (crises)

These are sudden crises that occur without warning and require change to cope with them. Examples might be a supplier going out of business, or a corporate take-over.

Improvement change (innovation)

Good managers see better, easier ways to do things all the time. They are constantly seeking and making improvements. Examples would be new product development, or introduction of new computer systems or programs.

Radical change (transformation)

This is where an organisation changes its entire way of doing things. It may be deliberate, or in response to a huge crisis.

Examples might be privatisation of a company, a merger, or closure of a part of the organisation.

Resistance to change

People' s natural response is often to resist change, because many people dislike change – they like things the way they are. Here are some of the main reasons for resistance to change.

~ Fear:
of experimenting
of failure
of looking silly
of loss of power
of loss of skills and/or expertise
of problems
of redundancy
of the unknown.

~ Lack:
of good working relationships
of information
of involvement
of security

of trust
of understanding the need for change.

~ Information issues:
erroneous information
ignorance
rumours.

~ Reasoning:
inflexibility
clinging to the status quo
erroneous thinking
habit
historical experience
inability to see the benefits
love of conformity.

Handling self-determined change

~ Define the problem or situation behind the need for change.

~ Gather information.

~ Create options.

~ Evaluate options.

~ Decide on the appropriate or best course

of action – what change to make and how.

- Implement your decision and make the change(s).
- Follow up and evaluate.

Handling imposed change

It is far harder to deal with changes that are imposed upon us than changes we originate ourselves. Many people will resist change, depending on circumstances, and resistance is more likely when change is imposed. *

Helping others through change

Overcoming resistance to change

Resistance to change can only be overcome through effort. Some people will come round in time, whilst others need to be helped.

Prepare people

- Be positive.
- Check for training needs.

** Change is something that happens every day, but that doesn't mean we like it. Some changes are tough to accept.*

- ~ Ensure adequate resources to make the change proceed smoothly.
- ~ Get the timing right where possible.
- ~ Set clear objectives.
- ~ Check that things which don't need to change are not affected.

Check information

- ~ Check facts before telling them to others
- ~ Check things out for yourself – look before you leap.
- ~ Keep people as informed as possible.
- ~ Tell people when you are not able to pass on information. Just knowing that *you* know what's going on may reassure them, even though you can't tell them!

Involve people

- ~ Ask for views and feedback.
- ~ Delegate where possible – this keeps people involved.

~ Get those affected to participate in decisions where possible.

~ Get to know people.

~ Involve experts – if anyone has specialist skills or expertise.

Communicate

~ Be honest.

~ Don't withhold information – tell people as much as you can.

~ Encourage two-way communication.

~ Explain the circumstances behind the change.

~ Make the change sound both achievable and sensible.

~ Sell people on the change – never try to force it on them.

Maintain awareness

~ Encourage others.

~ Stay aware of the progress of the change.

~ Recognise effort and contribution.

~ Recognise that resistance to change is healthy and natural, and may have to be tolerated before people can accept the change. *

~ Review and check that the change works.

~ Squash rumours wherever possible – preferably with facts.

Summary points

★ Always treat grievances seriously and objectively – whether or not you agree with them.

★ Handle disciplinary matters promptly and fairly. Be aware of the process and adhere to it.

★ Understand the reasons for change and how it affects people – including yourself.

★ Change takes time. Sometimes just managing people well through the process is all it takes to help them through.

** It's not that hard to overcome resistance to change or help people accept it. It just requires a little thought and empathy.*